THE JANE AUSTEN COLORING BOOK

THE JANE AUSTEN COLORING BOOK

ILLUSTRATED BY LUDOVIC SALLE

This edition published in 2022 by Sirius Publishing, a division of
Arcturus Publishing Limited,
26/27 Bickels Yard, 151–153 Bermondsey Street,
London SE1 3HA

ISBN: 978-1-3988-1469-1
CH010161NT
Supplier 29, Date 0522, PI 00000974

Printed in China

Created for children 10+

Introduction

The illustrations in this coloring book are based on or inspired by the works of Jane Austen and the time and place in which she lived and wrote. Some are scenes from her famous novels; others illustrate the fashions of the time, the places people visited, what they ate, and how they decorated their homes. They reflect the romance of the novels and the distinct fashions of the early 19th century—the Regency or Georgian era. Each illustration is accompanied by a quote from one of her novels.

Jane Austen was born on 16 December 1775 at Steventon, a small village in Hampshire, England. She received nearly all her education through her brothers and her father, an Anglican minister. Her earliest extant pieces date to 1787, when the author would have been 11 years of age. In adulthood, Austen began writing novels, though as her books were published anonymously—'BY A LADY'—she achieved little in the way of fame during her lifetime. That said, the identity of the author was known widely amongst the aristocracy. The Prince Regent, the future George IV, was a particular admirer of Austen's work. *Emma* was dedicated reluctantly to the prince at the urging of the author's friends. Although she wrote extensively on love and marriage, the author herself never wed, though she was briefly engaged—for a matter of hours—at the age of 26.

Sense and Sensibility began as *Elinor and Marianne*, Austen's first full-length novel, which is thought to have been written before 1796. She returned to the work late in 1797, revising it greatly. Published in 1811, when she was 35, *Sense and Sensibility* was a well-received work, selling out its print-run in under two years.

She started *Pride and Prejudice* in 1796, under the title *First Impressions*. Completed the following year, it became an Austen family favourite. The novel first appeared in print in 1813 and is the most beloved and funniest of Austen's novels. It concerns the considerable efforts of a couple, Mr and Mrs Bennet, to achieve suitable marriages for their five daughters. The focal point, however, is the relationship between the lively and intelligent Elizabeth Bennet and Mr Darcy, a man whom she initially dismisses as a cold and unfeeling aristocrat.

Mansfield Park came into being just months after the publication of *Sense and Sensibility*. Austen enjoyed her greatest commercial success with the novel. Launched in the summer of 1814, *Mansfield Park* earned more money than any other work published during her lifetime. *Emma* was first published in December 1815, days before the author's fortieth birthday. The work proved to be the last novel published during her lifetime.

Jane Austen began writing *Northanger Abbey* in the summer of 1798 and in 1803 the copyright in it was purchased for £10. In 1816, Austen reacquired the rights and immediately set about making revisions. She also started work on a new novel, *The Brothers*, in January 1817. But her health began to decline in the early months of 1816 and she was only able to work for the next three months. On 18 July 1817, she died in Winchester, where she had gone for medical treatment. *Northanger Abbey* and *Persuasion* were published five months later. Her final novel, *The Brothers*, was not published in full until 1925, as *Sanditon*.

To immerse yourself in the world of Jane Austen, find a peaceful place to work, take a selection of your favourite colored pencils, select an image, and choose a palette of colors to work with. You'll create a beautiful picture and find out more about the time and place in which Austen wrote her beloved novels.

It is a truth universally acknowledged, that a single man in possession of a good fortune must be in want of a wife.

Pride and Prejudice

'She is tolerable, but not handsome enough to tempt me; and I am in no humour at present to give consequence to young ladies who are slighted by other men. You had better return to your partner and enjoy her smiles, for you are wasting your time with me.'

Pride and Prejudice

'My idea of good company... is the company of clever, well-informed people, who have a great deal of conversation; that is what I call good company.'

'You are mistaken,' said he gently, 'that is not good company, that is the best.'

Persuasion

A·B·C·D·E·F·G·H·I·J·K·L·M·N·O·P·Q·R·S·T·U·V·W·X·Y·Z

Mr Hurst looked at her with astonishment.

'Do you prefer reading to cards?' said he; 'that is rather singular.'

'Miss Eliza Bennet,' said Miss Bingley, 'despises cards.
She is a great reader and has no pleasure in anything else.'

'I deserve neither such praise nor such censure,' cried Elizabeth;
'I am not a great reader, and I have pleasure in many things.'

Pride and Prejudice

Mr Denny addressed them directly, and entreated permission to introduce his friend, Mr Wickham, who had returned with him the day before from town, and he was happy to say had accepted a commission in their corps. This was exactly as it should be; for the young man wanted only regimentals to make him completely charming. His appearance was greatly in his favour; he had all the best part of beauty – a fine countenance, a good figure, and very pleasing address.

Pride and Prejudice

When coffee was over, Colonel Fitzwilliam reminded Elizabeth of having promised to play to him; and she sat down directly to the instrument. He drew a chair near her. Lady Catherine listened to half a song, and then talked, as before, to her other nephew; till the latter walked away from her, and moving with his usual deliberation towards the piano-forte, stationed himself so as to command a full view of the fair performer's countenance. Elizabeth saw what he was doing, and at the first convenient pause, turned to him with an arch smile, and said,

'You mean to frighten me, Mr Darcy, by coming in all this state to hear me?'

Pride and Prejudice

The first part of Mrs Gardiner's business on her arrival, was to distribute her presents and describe the newest fashions. When this was done, she had a less active part to play. It became her turn to listen. Mrs Bennet had many grievances to relate, and much to complain of. They had all been very ill-used since she last saw her sister. Two of her girls had been on the point of marriage, and after all there was nothing in it.

Pride and Prejudice

He had thought her wretchedly altered, and in the first moment of appeal, had spoken as he felt. He had not forgiven Anne Elliot. She had used him ill, deserted and disappointed him; and worse, she had shewn a feebleness of character in doing so, which his own decided, confident temper could not endure. She had given him up to oblige others. It had been the effect of over-persuasion. It had been weakness and timidity.

Persuasion

A gentleman carrying a gun, with two pointers playing round him, was passing up the hill and within a few yards of Marianne, when her accident happened. He put down his gun and ran to her assistance. She had raised herself from the ground, but her foot had been twisted in her fall, and she was scarcely able to stand. The gentleman offered his services; and perceiving that her modesty declined what her situation rendered necessary, took her up in his arms without farther delay, and carried her down the hill.

Sense and Sensibility

With what indignation such a letter as this must be read by Miss Dashwood, may be imagined. Though aware, before she began it, that it must bring a confession of his inconstancy, and confirm their separation for ever, she was not aware that such language could be suffered to announce it; nor could she have supposed Willoughby capable of departing so far from the appearance of every honourable and delicate feeling – so far from the common decorum of a gentleman, as to send a letter so impudently cruel: a letter which, instead of bringing with his desire of a release any professions of regret, acknowledged no breach of faith, denied all peculiar affection whatever – a letter of which every line was an insult, and which proclaimed its writer to be deep in hardened villainy.

Sense and Sensibility

... the eye was instantly caught by Pemberley House, situated on the opposite side of a valley, into which the road, with some abruptness, wound. It was a large, handsome, stone building, standing well on rising ground, and backed by a ridge of high woody hills; – and in front, a stream of some natural importance was swelled into greater, but without any artificial appearance. Its banks were neither formal, nor falsely adorned. Elizabeth was delighted. She had never seen a place for which nature had done more, or where natural beauty had been so little counteracted by an awkward taste.

Pride and Prejudice

Life seems but a quick succession of busy nothings.

Mansfield Park

If I could but know his heart, everything would become easy.

Sense and Sensibility

I really believe I shall always be talking of Bath,
when I am at home again – I do like it so very much.

Northanger Abbey

There could have been no two hearts so open,
no tastes so similar, no feelings so in unison.

Persuasion

One half of the world cannot understand the pleasures of the other.

Emma

Elinor found, when the evening was over, that disposition is not materially altered by a change of abode, for although scarcely settled in town, Sir John had contrived to collect around him, nearly twenty young people, and to amuse them with a ball.

Sense and Sensibility

Dear Diary, Today I tried not to think about Mr. Knightly. I tried not to think about him when I discussed the menu with Cook ... I tried not to think about him in the garden where I thrice plucked the petals off a daisy to ascertain his feelings for Harriet. I don't think we should keep daisies in the garden, they really are a drab little flower. And I tried not to think about him when I went to bed, but something had to be done.

Emma

Mary wished to say something very sensible, but knew not how.

Pride and Prejudice

'Oh! very well,' exclaimed Miss Bates, 'then I need not be uneasy.

'Three things very dull indeed.' That will just do for me, you know. I shall be sure to say three dull things as soon as ever I open my mouth, shan't I? (looking round with the most good-humoured dependence on every body's assent) – Do not you all think I shall?'

Emma could not resist.

'Ah! ma'am, but there may be a difficulty. Pardon me – but you will be limited as to number – only three at once.'

Miss Bates, deceived by the mock ceremony of her manner, did not immediately catch her meaning; but, when it burst on her, it could not anger, though a slight blush shewed that it could pain her.

Emma

The more I know of the world, the more I am convinced that I shall never see a man whom I can really love. I require so much!

Sense and Sensibility

A lady's imagination is very rapid; it jumps from admiration to love, from love to matrimony in a moment.

Pride and Prejudice

The hardness of the pavement for her feet, made him less willing upon the present occasion; he did it, however; she was safely down, and instantly, to shew her enjoyment, ran up the steps to be jumped down again. He advised her against it, thought the jar too great; but no, he reasoned and talked in vain; she smiled and said, 'I am determined I will:' he put out his hands; she was too precipitate by half a second, she fell on the pavement on the Lower Cobb, and was taken up lifeless!

Persuasion

'Vanity and pride are different things, though the words are often used synonymously. A person may be proud without being vain. Pride relates more to our opinion of ourselves, vanity to what we would have others think of us.'

Pride and Prejudice

These two girls had been above an hour in the place, happily employed in visiting an opposite milliner, watching the sentinel on guard, and dressing a salad and cucumber.

Pride and Prejudice

'Do you know, I saw the prettiest hat you can imagine, in a shop window in Milsom Street just now – very like yours, only with coquelicot ribbons instead of green; I quite longed for it.'

Northanger Abbey

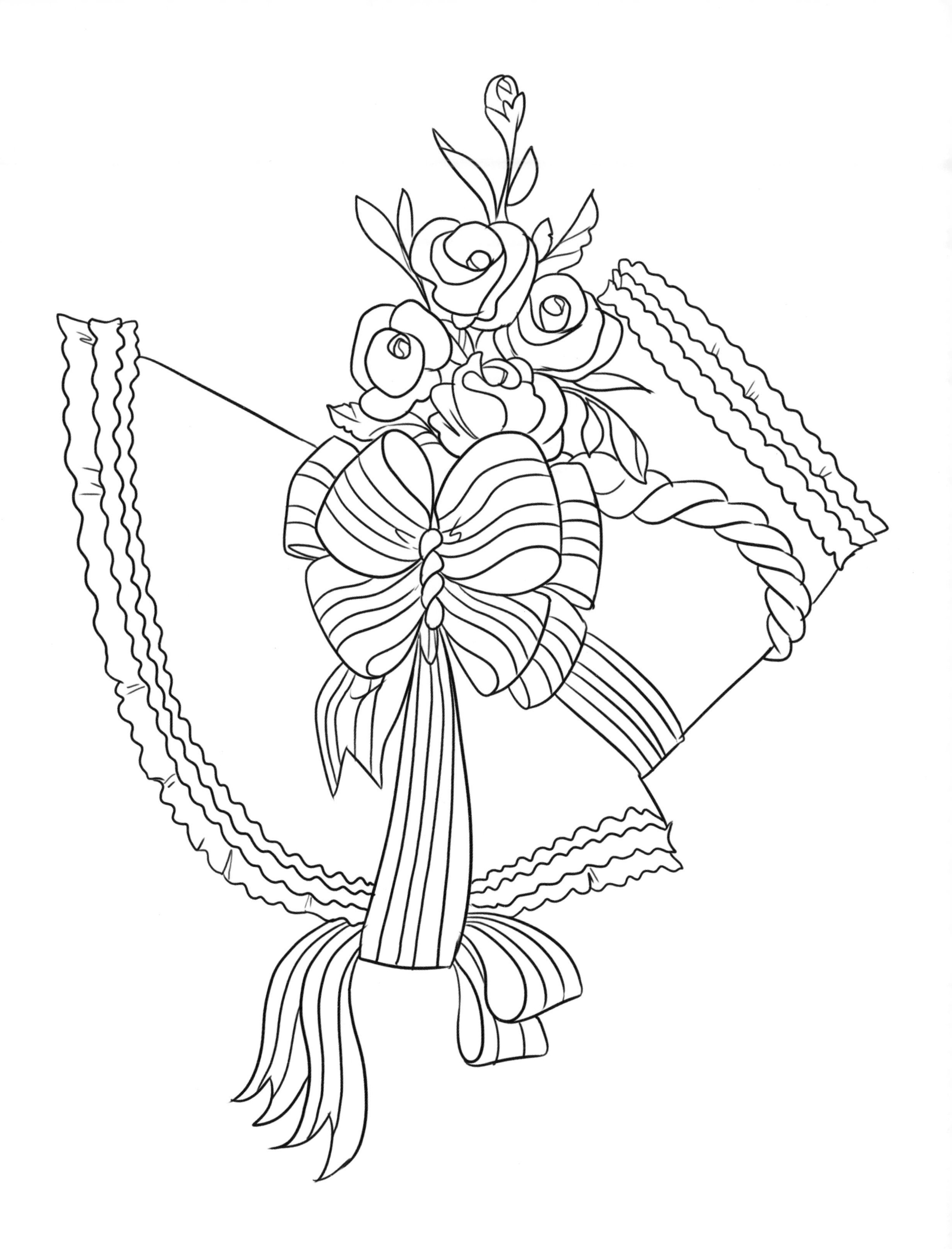

If adventures will not befall a young lady in her own village, she must seek them abroad.

Northanger Abbey

It is very right that you should go to town; I would have every young woman of your condition in life acquainted with the manners and amusements of London.

Sense and Sensibility

The plan of the young couple was to proceed, after a few days, to Brighton, and take a house there for some weeks. Every public place was new to Maria, and Brighton is almost as gay in winter as in summer.

Mansfield Park

'If one could but go to Brighton!' observed Mrs Bennet.

'Oh, yes! If one could but go to Brighton! But papa is so disagreeable.'

Pride and Prejudice

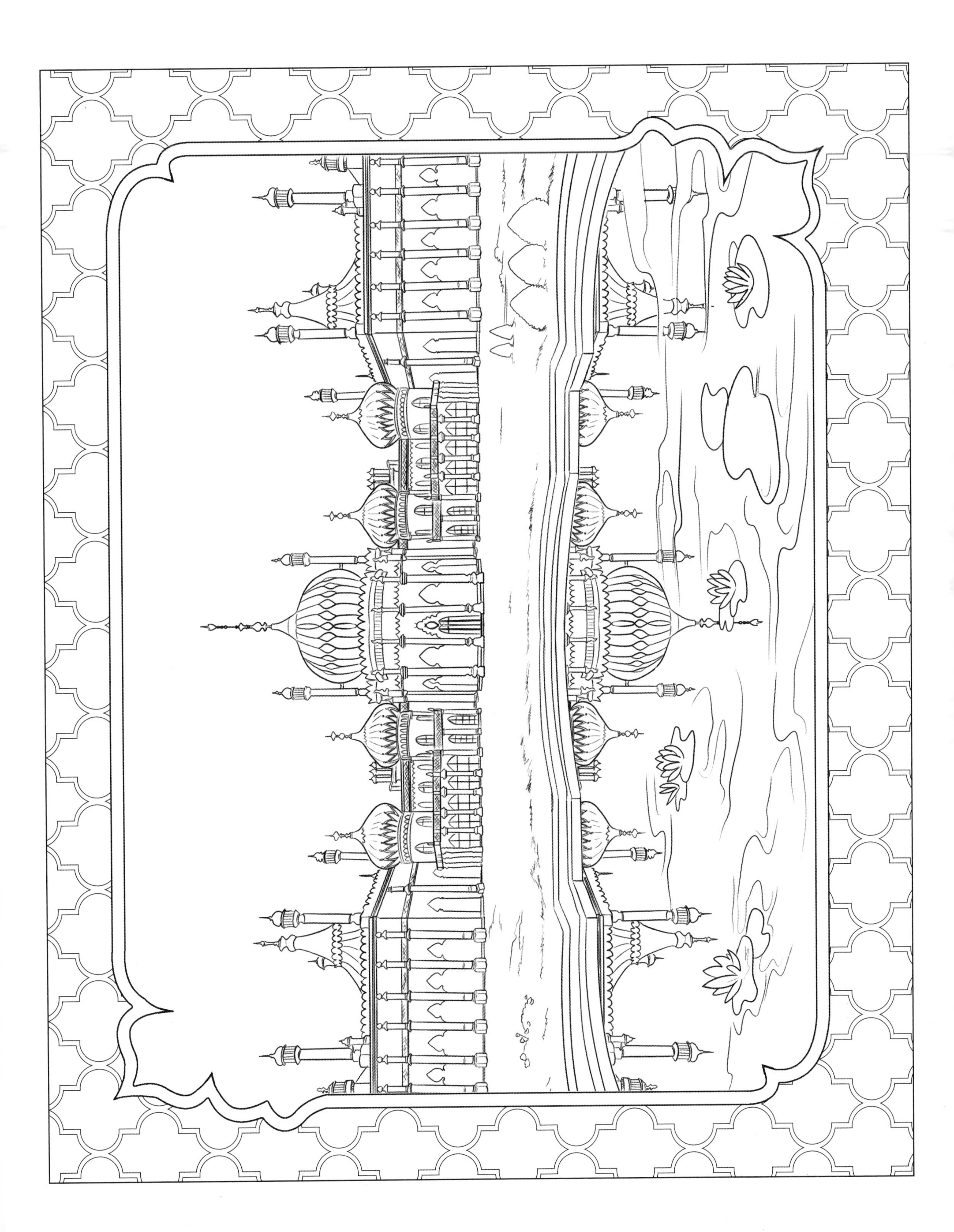

I never in my life saw anything more elegant than their dresses.

Pride and Prejudice

It soon led to another; and Mrs. Bennet found, with amazement and horror, that her husband would not advance a guinea to buy clothes for his daughter.

Pride and Prejudice

One man's ways may be as good as another's,
but we all like our own best.

Persuasion

'A little sea-bathing would set me up for ever.'

Pride and Prejudice

Why not seize the pleasure at once?

How often is happiness destroyed by preparation, foolish preparation!

Emma

BooKshop

A house was never taken good care of, Mr Shepherd observed, without a lady: he did not know, whether furniture might not be in danger of suffering as much where there was no lady, as where there were many children.

Persuasion

We three shall be able to go very well in my chaise; and when we are in town, if you do not like to go wherever I do, well and good, you may always go with one of my daughters.

Sense and Sensibility

'Follies and nonsense, whims and inconsistencies do divert me,
I own, and I laugh at them whenever I can.'

Pride and Prejudice

'No, indeed, I should not. I do not pretend to say that I was not very much pleased with him; but while I have Udolpho *to read, I feel as if nobody could make me miserable. Oh! The dreadful black veil! My dear Isabella, I am sure there must be Laurentina's skeleton behind it.'*

'It is so odd to me, that you should never have read Udolpho before; but I suppose Mrs Morland objects to novels.'

Northanger Abbey

If he had a hobby-horse, it was that. He loved a garden. Though careless enough in most matters of eating, he loved good fruit – or if he did not, his friends and children did. There were great vexations, however, attending such a garden as his. The utmost care could not always secure the most valuable fruits. The pinery had yielded only one hundred in the last year.

Northanger Abbey

... man only can be aware of the insensibility of man towards a new gown ... Woman is fine for her satisfaction alone. No man will admire her the more, no woman will like her the better for it.

Northanger Abbey

'John is in such spirits to-day!' said she, on his taking Miss Steele's pocket handkerchief, and throwing it out of the window – 'He is full of monkey tricks.' And soon afterwards, on the second boy's violently pinching one of the same lady's fingers, she fondly observed, 'How playful William is!'

Northanger Abbey

She had been forced into prudence in her youth, she learned romance as she grew older: the natural sequel of an unnatural beginning.

Persuasion

Afraid of every body, ashamed of herself, and longing for the home she had left, she knew not how to look up, and could scarcely speak to be heard, or without crying ... In vain were the well-meant condescensions of Sir Thomas, and all the officious prognostications of Mrs Norris that she would be a good girl; in vain did Lady Bertram smile and make her sit on the sofa with herself and Pug, and vain was even the sight of a gooseberry tart towards giving her comfort; she could scarcely swallow two mouthfuls before tears interrupted her, and sleep seeming to be her likeliest friend, she was taken to finish her sorrows in bed.

Mansfield Park

After some minutes spent in this way, Miss Bertram, observing the iron gate, expressed a wish of passing through it into the park, that their views and their plans might be more comprehensive. It was the very thing of all others to be wished, it was the best, it was the only way of proceeding with any advantage, in Henry Crawford's opinion; and he directly saw a knoll not half a mile off, which would give them exactly the requisite command of the house. Go therefore they must to that knoll, and through that gate; but the gate was locked. Mr Rushworth wished he had brought the key; he had been very near thinking whether he should not bring the key; he was determined he would never come without the key again; but still this did not remove the present evil ... it ended in Mr Rushworth's declaring outright that he would go and fetch the key. He set off accordingly.

Mansfield Park

Fanny had a good deal of enjoyment in the course of the evening; but Henry's attentions had very little to do with it. She would much rather not have been asked by him again so very soon, and she wished she had not been obliged to suspect that his previous inquiries of Mrs Norris, about the supper hour, were all for the sake of securing her at that part of the evening. But it was not to be avoided: he made her feel that she was the object of all; though she could not say that it was unpleasantly done, that there was indelicacy or ostentation in his manner; and sometimes, when he talked of William, he was really not unagreeable, and shewed even a warmth of heart which did him credit. But still his attentions made no part of her satisfaction.

Mansfield Park

On her father, her confidence had not been sanguine, but he was more negligent of his family, his habits were worse, and his manners coarser, than she had been prepared for. He did not want abilities but he had no curiosity, and no information beyond his profession; he read only the newspaper and the navy-list; he talked only of the dockyard, the harbour, Spithead, and the Motherbank; he swore and he drank, he was dirty and gross. She had never been able to recall anything approaching to tenderness in his former treatment of herself. There had remained only a general impression of roughness and loudness; and now he scarcely ever noticed her, but to make her the object of a coarse joke.

Mansfield Park

'Miss Bennet, do you know who I am? I have not been accustomed to such language as this. I am almost the nearest relation he has in the world, and am entitled to know all his dearest concerns.'

'But you are not entitled to know mine; nor will such behaviour as this ever induce me to be explicit.'

'Let me be rightly understood. This match, to which you have the presumption to aspire, can never take place. No, never. Mr Darcy is engaged to my daughter. Now what have you to say?'

Pride and Prejudice

Mr Collins was not a sensible man, and the deficiency of nature had been but little assisted by education or society; the greatest part of his life having been spent under the guidance of an illiterate and miserly father; and though he belonged to one of the universities, he had merely kept the necessary terms, without forming at it any useful acquaintance.

Pride and Prejudice

'Ah! There is nothing like staying at home, for real comfort.'

Emma

'Mr Darcy was punctual in his return, and as Lydia informed you, attended the wedding. He dined with us the next day, and was to leave town again on Wednesday or Thursday. Will you be very angry with me, my dear Lizzy, if I take this opportunity of saying (what I was never bold enough to say before) how much I like him. His behaviour to us has, in every respect, been as pleasing as when we were in Derbyshire.'

Pride and Prejudice

'I assure you that if Darcy were not such a great tall fellow, in comparison with myself, I should not pay him half so much deference. I declare I do not know a more aweful object than Darcy, on particular occasions, and in particular places; at his own house especially, and of a Sunday evening when he has nothing to do.'

Pride and Prejudice

To look almost *pretty is an acquisition of higher delight to a girl who has been looking plain the first fifteen years of her life than a beauty from her cradle can ever receive.*

Northanger Abbey

'I assure you. I have no notion of treating men with such respect. That is the way to spoil them.'

Northanger Abbey

'Silly things do cease to be silly if they are done by sensible people in an impudent way.'

Emma

The elegance of the breakfast set forced itself on Catherine's notice when they were seated at table ... He was enchanted by her approbation of his taste, confessed it to be neat and simple, thought it right to encourage the manufacture of his country; and for his part, to his uncritical palate, the tea was as well flavoured from the clay of Staffordshire, as from that of Dresden [Germany] or Save [France].

Northanger Abbey

'I cannot make speeches, Emma ... If I loved you less, I might be able to talk about it more. But you know what I am. You hear nothing but truth from me. I have blamed you, and lectured you, and you have borne it as no other woman in England would have borne it.'

Emma

'I could not be happy with a man whose taste did not in every point coincide with my own. He must enter in all my feelings; the same books, the same music must charm us both.'

Sense and Sensibility

Her Bath habits made evening-parties perfectly natural to her, and Maple Grove had given her a taste for dinners. She was a little shocked at the want of two drawing rooms, at the poor attempt at rout-cakes, and there being no ice in the Highbury card parties.

Emma